MW01616781

SEASONS

**HOW GOD LEADS US
THROUGH CHANGE**

PRESENTED TO

BY

DATE

Lifeway Press®
Brentwood, Tennessee

ISBN 978-1-0877-8493-9
Item 005842365
Dewey Decimal Classification Number: 242
Subject Heading: DEVOTIONAL LITERATURE / BIBLE STUDY AND TEACHING / GOD

Printed in the United States of America.

Student Ministry Publishing
Lifeway Resources
200 Powell Place, Suite 100
Brentwood, Tennessee 37027

We believe that the Bible has God for its author; salvation for its end; truth, without any mixture of error, for its matter; and that all Scripture is totally true and trustworthy. To review Lifeway's doctrinal guideline, please visit https://www.lifeway.com/about/doctrinal-guidelines.

PUBLISHING TEAM

Director, Next Gen Ministries
Chuck Peters

Manager, Small Group Resources
Karen Daniel

Writer
Melanie Gillen

Content Editor
Kyle Wiltshire

Production Editor
April-Lyn Caouette

Graphic Designer
Shiloh Stufflebeam

TABLE OF CONTENTS

INTRO

There's nothing quite like the beginning of a new season. The freshness of spring, summer vacation, the crisp fall air, and the coziness of winter—each season offers such unique delights. And just as nature's seasons change, there are seasons of life where we will experience change. Some of these are changes we welcome, but there are some we would rather not experience. Fortunately, one thing we can count on is that Jesus is right there with us as we navigate all the changes in our lives.

In a world of change, it's comforting to know that there's something (and Someone) that will always stay the same: God and His love for you. You can always rest in Him, no matter what you experience or face in life.

Somehow you ended up with this devotional in your hand today. You may have picked it up due to some transitions you've gone through lately, or someone may have given it to you as a tool to help guide you through a new season in your life. Regardless of how you ended up with this book, I pray that God uses it to not only give you hope and encouragement but also to help you fall more in love with Jesus, the One who never changes.

Before you begin this thirty-day journey, take a moment to pray that God will open your heart as you dig into His Word. I pray you will forever be changed because of Jesus!

GETTING STARTED

This devotional contains thirty days of content, broken down into sections. Each day is divided into three elements—**discover**, **delight**, and **display**—to help you grow in your faith.

DISCOVER

This section helps you examine the verses in light of who God is and determine what they say about your identity in relationship to Him. Included here is the daily Scripture reading and key verses, along with illustrations and commentary to guide you as you learn more about God's Word.

DELIGHT

In this section, you'll be challenged by questions and activities that help you see how God is alive and active in every detail of His Word and your life.

DISPLAY

Here's where you take action. This section calls you to apply what you've learned through each day.

Each day also includes a prayer guide at the conclusion of the devotion.

Throughout the devotional, you'll also find extra items to help you connect with the topic personally, such as Scripture memory verses and interactive articles.

WHEN CHANGE IS GOOD

SOMETIMES WE WELCOME CHANGE IN OUR LIVES. WHETHER IT'S GETTING OUR DRIVER'S LICENSE, GETTING OUR BRACES OFF, FINALLY PULLING OUR MATH GRADE UP, OR ONE DAY GETTING MARRIED, THERE ARE LIFE CHANGES THAT ARE GOOD AND WELCOMED. IN THIS SECTION, WE'LL EXPLORE HOW WE GROW IN OUR RELATIONSHIP WITH GOD AS WE EXPERIENCE THE GOOD AND NEEDED CHANGES IN OUR LIVES.

From Death to Life

READ 2 CORINTHIANS 5:16-21.

Therefore, if anyone is in Christ, he is a new creation;
the old has passed away, and see, the new has come!
— 2 Corinthians 5:17

DISCOVER

Change is inevitable. From friends, to trends, to our plans, things in life are constantly evolving. Some people thrive with change, while others hate it. However, there is only one change in our lives that will affect eternity—the decision to follow Jesus. It is the most important decision and it leads to the best change you could ever make. Nothing else can top it because Jesus takes us from death to life, from a hopeless life to a hopeful one.

God created a perfect and beautiful world. Unfortunately, Adam and Eve introduced sin to the world through their disobedience (see Gen. 3). This caused a separation between us and our Creator. But because of His great love for us, He provided a way for us to be united with Him once again: Jesus. God sent His only Son to earth to live a perfect life. When Jesus died on the cross, He did it so that our relationship with God could be restored.

That leaves us with a choice. Will we choose to follow Jesus? Will we choose to live under His authority? In 2 Corinthians 5:17, we find a promise that if anyone places his or her faith in Jesus and has a relationship with Him, that person is a new creation. It doesn't matter what you've done or what background you come from—when God does His saving work in your life, He changes you. It is the most important change you will ever experience!

Has there been a time in your life when you decided to follow Jesus? If there has, take a minute to write about how you came into a relationship with Him. If you have not decided to follow Jesus, what's holding you back?

Are you sharing with others about the change Jesus has made in you? What are some ways you could share Jesus with the people you encounter every day?

DISPLAY

Our faith is something that shouldn't be hidden. How can you tell others about the change from death to life that you have experienced? People love a good story. Consider sharing the story of your salvation with a friend this week. Sharing your story of faith with your friends is the most loving thing you can do. It may be intimidating, but you can pray for boldness as you share about the transforming work of Jesus in your life.

Father, thank You for Your saving work on the cross. Thank You for making the most meaningful change in my life. You brought me from death to life, and I am forever grateful. I pray that I can always remember what You have done in my life and then help others to have the same experience. Help me step out in boldness to share with my friends about the difference You have made in my life. I do not want to keep the story of Your goodness to myself. I pray that lives are forever changed for You. Thank You, Jesus!

Growing Up

READ LUKE 2:41-52.

And Jesus increased in wisdom and stature,
and in favor with God and with people.
— Luke 2:52

DISCOVER

It's comforting to know that even Jesus went through changes in His life. At the time of these verses, Jesus was twelve years old. He was entering into His teenage years, growing and changing just like you are. Jesus is the model of perfection, so as we look at how He grew throughout His life, we can see the areas in which we should be growing in maturity as well.

According to Luke 2:52, Jesus grew **mentally**. He spent time in the temple, learning and seeking to understand. He wasn't just becoming smarter—He was learning to apply that knowledge in His life.

Jesus also grew **physically**. He had growth spurts, just like you do! He was getting taller and stronger as He grew older. Jesus may not have spent hours at the gym, but He made sure to work hard to become strong.

Jesus grew **spiritually**. His relationship with God was being strengthened and matured. He was close to His Father. We see in Scripture that He spent time praying to God.

Lastly, Jesus grew **socially**. He was developing His relationships with others. He showed genuine love and care for those He interacted with. As He grew, He also developed a core group of friends with whom He spent much of His time.

Just as Jesus grew in these areas, we should seek to grow as well.

Look at your life. Are you growing and changing to become more like Jesus? In the spaces below, write ways you are growing in all the areas that Jesus grew.

Mentally:

Physically:

Spiritually:

Socially:

DISPLAY

Our walk with Jesus should always be changing and growing as we become more like Him. The people around Jesus could tell that He was growing and maturing. Do you think the people in your life can see growth in you? If there are areas in your life where you would like to grow more, consider who can help you. In the space below, write the area you want to grow in and who can help you grow in that space.

Lord, thank You for giving me the perfect example of how to grow in my walk with You and in life. Please allow me to set aside my pride and take an honest look at the growth in my life. Guide and direct me as I take the next step of obedience in following You. A life spent with You is better than anything!

Transformed

READ ROMANS 12:1-2.

*Do not be conformed to this age, but be transformed by
the renewing of your mind, so that you may discern what is
the good, pleasing, and perfect will of God.*
— Romans 12:2

DISCOVER

It is easy to conform to the world. According to CNN, teens today are
spending an average of seven hours a day looking at screens (and that's
not including school work).[1] Excessive screen time can cause depression
and anxiety, and it can impact social development. You may not be looking
at a screen that much right now, but even if you don't, culture has a way of
seeping in and making us conform to the patterns of the world. If we aren't
intentional about our walk with Jesus, we begin to drift away from God.

God calls us to continual transformation. We shouldn't follow what the
world has to offer but focus our eyes on Jesus. We are transformed by the
renewal of our minds, but how? It's simple: we spend time in the Word! We
will never be spiritually mature without spending time with Jesus.

Did you know that flamingos aren't born pink? They're actually born
with gray or white feathers, and their color transforms with age because
of chemicals called carotenoids in the foods they eat. As they mature,
they become the beautiful shade of pink we're familiar with. For us,
transformation from one thing to another happens as we spend time
in God's Word and in prayer. The Word of God is living and active, and
when we fill ourselves with it, we can't help but be changed. We no longer
conform to the patterns of the world and we are transformed to become
more of who God has called us to be.

1 Kristen Rogers, "US Teens Use Screens More Than Seven Hours a Day on Average - and That's
Not Including School Work," CNN, October 29, 2019, https://www.cnn.com/2019/10/29/health/
common-sense-kids-media-use-report-wellness/index.html.

To renew our minds, we need to make an active decision to allow God to transform us. Do you have a plan on how you can allow Him to renew your mind daily? If you do, what is it? If not, develop a plan now.

Think about the times in your past when you were closest to the Lord. What was happening during those times?

DISPLAY

Nothing in life is more transformational than time with Jesus. We know we need to spend time with Him, but sometimes it's a challenge. One way you can keep yourself on track is by finding a friend to help you stay accountable. Who comes to mind?

Consider doing a reading plan with this friend. You could easily pick a book of the Bible to read together. There are also free plans online or in Bible reading apps. You could pick a devotional to go through together. You could all join a group where you study Scripture together and then discuss it through a group text. The time you spend with Jesus is never wasted. God will use that time to make you more like Him!

Lord, thank You for transforming my heart and life. I pray that I would keep my eyes fixed on You as I walk through life. Help me to be continuously transformed by Your Word rather than by what the world offers. I long to spend time with You—please bring friends into my life who encourage me to pursue You more. I pray that we would keep each other accountable to spend time with You so that we can be transformed to be more like Jesus.

New Body

READ 1 CORINTHIANS 15:50-58.

Listen, I am telling you a mystery: We will not all fall asleep,
but we will all be changed, in a moment, in the twinkling of an eye,
at the last trumpet. For the trumpet will sound, and the dead
will be raised incorruptible, and we will be changed.
— 1 Corinthians 15:51-52

DISCOVER

I love good mysteries. In most mystery movies I have watched, if you pay attention, there are little clues that are easy to miss. Typically, if I watch the movie a second time, I can see the clues that I missed the first time.

When the Bible speaks of a mystery, it means we should pay attention, because there's something for us to learn spiritually. We don't want to miss what God has for us. In today's verses, we can learn something important about the change that will inevitably happen in our lives when we die.

When Paul refers to "sleep" in today's verses, he isn't talking about taking a nap. This is a gentle way to talk about the death of a believer. Paul says that when we die, "we will be changed" (v. 52). That makes sense; death is obviously a change. However, he's talking about something much bigger than the stopping of our hearts. For believers, our death causes a change in our lives that is beautiful. Although our physical bodies do not go to heaven when we die, we will receive new heavenly bodies when Jesus returns.

None of us know what these new bodies will look like, but Scripture shows us that our heavenly bodies will be free from pain, decay, and age. Our sinful nature will no longer apply to our physical state. Although we don't know when the Lord will return, we do know that when He does, believers will experience the change of the resurrection. We will be raised like Jesus and receive new bodies that will never grow old!

What does living with an eternal perspective look like in your life?

Write out a prayer to God thanking Him for Your earthly body and then for your future heavenly body.

DISPLAY

It's so easy for us to become frustrated with things in this fallen world. Sin has corrupted God's perfect design. Our bodies are never what we hope they will be. Either you or someone close to you will experience sickness or disease. Our teeth often need braces, and our eyes often need glasses.

However, if we live lives focused on eternity with Jesus and the change that will one day happen, we will have hope. I have heard it said that a good definition of the word hope can be found in the following acrostic: "Hold On: Pain Ends." It sure will.

Hang on, friends. We know the victor. Pain will end, and we will experience a holy transformation one day. Write the above acrostic for hope on a note card and place it somewhere you will see it often. Let it serve as a reminder to hold on, because pain ends.

Father, what an incredible place heaven will be. As I eagerly anticipate a lifetime of sitting at Your feet and praising Your name, help me to use my time here on earth to share Your love and Your truth. You have put me here, and although this place isn't perfect, I know You are. I place my hope in You.

Each Step Counts

READ EPHESIANS 5:15-21.

*Pay careful attention, then, to how you walk —
not as unwise people but as wise.
—Ephesians 5:15*

DISCOVER

Have you ever been hiking? Sometimes the trail can have roots and branches that cover the places where you are trying to walk. You have to be incredibly careful about how and where you take your steps, or inevitably, you will trip. I've seen too many people bite it on the trails because they weren't paying attention.

Just like when we're hiking on treacherous ground, we need to be careful about how we walk with Jesus. The wise people of the world will change and be intentional about their steps. We need to pay attention. Although it may be humorous to watch someone fall harmlessly on a hike, there isn't anything funny about a person who messes up in life because that person wasn't aware of what God was trying to do in his or her life.

We have one life to live here on earth. How we spend our time matters. How can we use the time we have been given in the best way possible? We change. We don't do the things that the unwise do. We rely on Jesus to help make us wise. The wise understand what the will of the Lord is: for us to bring Him glory! What are some markers of those who are wise and are bringing God glory? They are filled with the Spirit. They are joyful and have gratitude for all that God has done for them. They don't get caught up in arguments with others but submit to each other so they can keep their eyes fixed on Jesus.

Walk carefully. Pay attention to the path that God is leading you down. If you happen to trip, get up, seek forgiveness, and keep walking!

What small steps can you make to walk towards Jesus this week?

What are some areas in your life where you are walking unwisely? What steps can you take to eliminate these unwise things from your walk?

As believers, we are called to live lives that bring God glory. We do that by living lives of intention—and that often requires us to do things differently than we did before. If we give our attention and time to Jesus, we will be changed. However, if most of our focus goes to our phones, internet memes, cat videos, and things of the world, we will instead become like those things we give our attention to. We already know that change happens in our lives when we spend time with Jesus. The more we spend time with Him, the more we become like Him. If we are going to live lives that glorify Him, it won't happen by accident. What we focus on matters.

Take some time to write out what you've paid attention to in the last twenty-hour hours. Are you shocked by how you spend your time? The good news is that you can easily change your priorities. Ask God to help you as you prioritize Jesus in your life.

Father, I desire to live a life worthy of the gospel. Thank You for giving us a blueprint for walking wisely. As I walk with You, help me to pay attention to what You have for me. When I trip, help me to get back up again. Thank You for walking beside me. It is comforting to know that I do not have to do this alone.

Put Your Yes on the Table

READ GENESIS 12:1-9.

I will bless those who bless you, I will curse anyone who treats you with contempt, and all the peoples on earth will be blessed through you.
— Genesis 12:3

DISCOVER

God asked Abram to leave his country and his people and to travel to an undisclosed land. Talk about a huge change. I don't like it when I have to change where I sit at church, let alone leave everything I've grown to love. Yet, in verse 4, we see that Abram went, just as the Lord told Him. I am sure he had his questions, but his faith caused him to obey and move.

There will be times when God asks us to do very brave and bold things for Him. However, He also asks us to make slight changes that bring Him glory. He may ask you to show kindness to a kid at school or hold a door open for someone. He may ask you to do some extra chores around the house or share the gospel with a friend. It's often the small acts of obedience that open the door for bigger movements of God. Abram already had his yes on the table when God asked him to move.

Abram's act of obedience paved the way for the biggest blessing of all: Jesus. Abram may not have known exactly what the next stage of life would look like for him, but he trusted God and walked in faith. As we read Scripture, we see that Abram's life was marked by decisions of obedience and changes that he had to face (see Gen. 22). Our lives will also be marked by the obedient steps of faith we will take.

Is your yes on the table? Are you willing to go where God is calling you to go or do what He is calling you to do? How do you know?

If your yes is not on the table yet, what is stopping you from being all in on whatever His plans are for you?

DISPLAY

Change is hard, but God may be asking you to do some things differently in your life. What would it look like to put your yes on the table? Your obedience could drastically change your school, friendships, sports teams, church, and family. We don't need to know all the answers, but we must be willing to say yes when God asks us to move. Where is God calling you to say yes to Him in your life today?

Lord, thank You for working in my life. Even when I don't see Your hand, I can trust Your heart. Help me to follow You with everything in me. I want to move when You tell me to move. Help me to take the small steps of obedience in my walk with You.

MEMORY VERSES

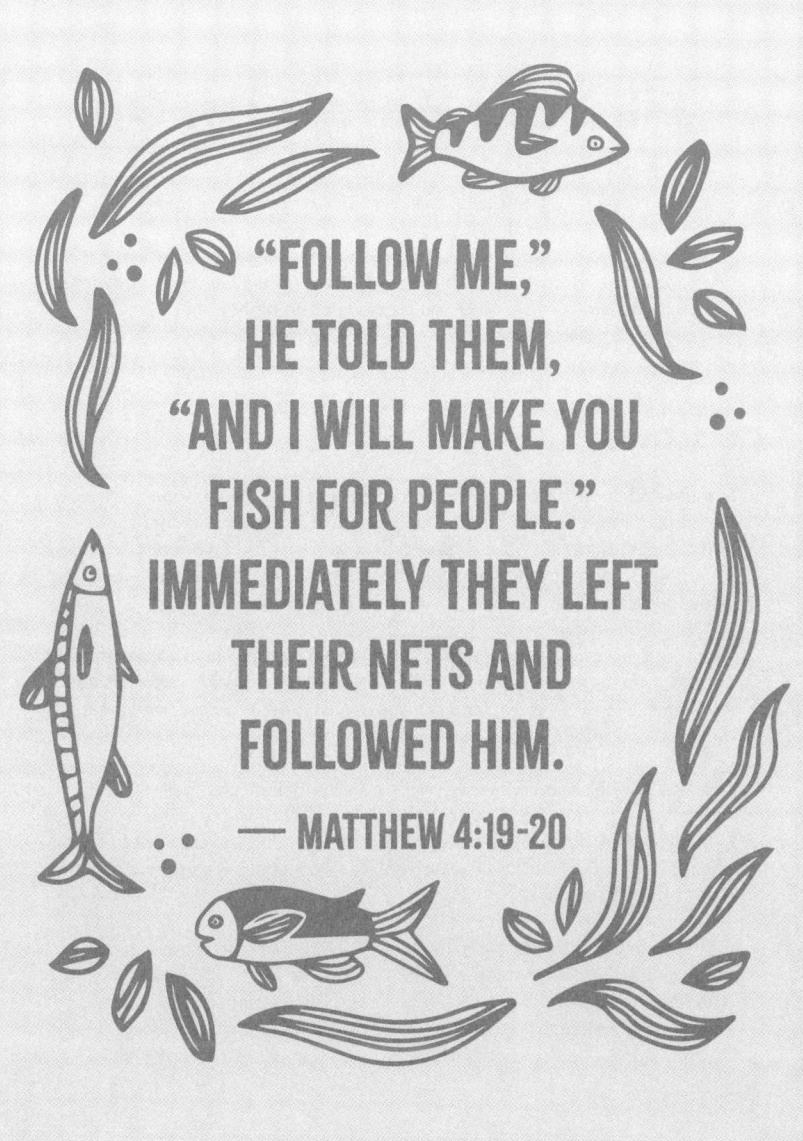

"FOLLOW ME,"
HE TOLD THEM,
"AND I WILL MAKE YOU
FISH FOR PEOPLE."
IMMEDIATELY THEY LEFT
THEIR NETS AND
FOLLOWED HIM.

— MATTHEW 4:19-20

Fill Your Horn with Oil

READ 1 SAMUEL 16:1-13.

*The LORD said to Samuel, "How long are you going to mourn
for Saul, since I have rejected him as king over Israel? Fill your horn with oil
and go. I am sending you to Jesse of Bethlehem because
I have selected for myself a king from his sons."*
— 1 Samuel 16:1

DISCOVER

Samuel had spent so much time and energy helping Saul become the king.
He had anointed Saul as the first king of Israel, and he was a mentor to
him. Despite Samuel's hopes, having Saul as king didn't work out, and God
asked him to find another king. As you can imagine, Samuel was upset. He
grieved the fact that Saul would no longer be the king.

Then the Lord gave Samuel a pep talk. He told him to fill his horn with oil
and go. He was essentially saying "Listen, I know things are not what you
expected, but we have work to do. We can sit here and pout, or we can
move on and anoint another king."

Just like Samuel, sometimes we don't want to make a change—we like
things the way they are. Maybe we're afraid of putting ourselves out there
in a vulnerable way. Maybe we were hurt before, and the thought of trying
again brings us anxiety. Maybe we feel like we just don't want to do what
God is calling us to do

God may ask you to make a hard change. With God's help, we can do
hard things. God did not leave Samuel to go out alone. He told him what
to bring. When Samuel expressed his fears, God provided. Making the
change that we know we need to make can be hard, but God doesn't let
us do it alone. We do it with His help.

What hard changes has God asked you to make? What was hard about these different things?

What do you think holds you back from doing what God has asked you to do? What are some practical steps you could take today to help you move forward with the changes God is asking you to make?

DISPLAY

Change is hard. I once heard the following statement: "Everything is hard until it's not." Pushing ourselves into doing something new or learning something new can be hard. But the more we work at it, the easier it becomes. The same can be said for doing what God wants us to do. Sometimes, the hardest step is the first one. Once we take that first step, the following steps are a little easier. I do not know what kind of change you need to make today, but chances are, you do.

Fill your horn with oil and go. Take the first step today that God is calling you to make.

Father, thank You for inviting me to be included in Your plan. Show me the changes that I need to make, then fill me with Your strength as I walk in obedience to You. I pray that You take away the obstacles that are holding me back and help me to push forward with strength and boldness.

DAY 8

Follow Me

READ MATTHEW 4:18-22.

"Follow me," he told them, "and I will make you fish for people."
Immediately they left their nets and followed him.
— Matthew 4:19-20

DISCOVER

It was a normal day for two sets of brothers: Simon and Andrew, and James and John. They were busy working, doing what they always did— fishing. As they were casting and mending their nets, Jesus called out to them and gave them an invitation to follow Him. They immediately dropped their nets and followed Him.

Scripture shows us several examples of times when God called people out when they are already busy doing something. God called David as he was shepherding his flock. He called Moses when he was looking after the flock of his father-in-law. Matthew was working as a tax collector when Jesus called him to follow.

God tends to call us when we are already in motion. So many times, we don't know what God wants us to do in life, but it is important to do *something*. If we're just sitting around and waiting for God to move, we may be waiting a while. If you don't know what to do next, faithfully keep doing the last thing that God told you to do until He says to stop.

How is God being glorified through your life, even in times of waiting?

What things in your life do you have trouble leaving behind as you follow Jesus?

DISPLAY

If you don't feel like God is calling you to make a change now, stop and pray that He would open your eyes to what He wants you to do. In the meantime, continue doing what you already know He wants you to do. By faithfully pursuing Jesus daily, you will be ready when God calls you to move in a new direction. This change will not only bring Him glory but will also give you peace and direction.

Jesus, thank You that You are still calling people to follow You. Thank You for the invitation You have given me to follow You. Help me to consistently bring You glory so that when You call me to the next adventure, I will be ready.

DAY 9

Second Chance

READ ACTS 15:36-41.

*They had such a sharp disagreement that they parted company, and
Barnabas took Mark with him and sailed off to Cyprus.*
— Acts 15:39

DISCOVER

It would be easy to focus on the argument between Paul and Barnabas in
these verses. I mean, goodness, these guys had a huge blow-out argument
over Mark, and it's human nature to want to watch a fight. But instead of
focusing on the fight, we should look at what they were fighting over.

Paul and Barnabas were getting ready to set out on their second
missionary journey, intending to check in with all the churches they had
planted and encourage them. Barnabas thought it would be a good idea
to take Mark, but Paul didn't like that plan. Mark had messed up—he
had abandoned them on their last journey, and Paul didn't want to risk it
happening again. Barnabas thought Mark needed a second chance. This
led to a big fight. Even though the two didn't throw punches, they couldn't
come to an agreement, and they parted ways. Barnabas went one way and
took Mark with him. Paul chose Silas and headed toward Syria.

Sometimes hard decisions end up bringing needed change. When Paul
and Barnabas separated under not-so-pleasant terms, they were able to
double their mission to help strengthen the churches that they had planted.
This change also helped lead to Mark's restoration.

Barnabas knew that Mark deserved a second chance. Because of that,
Mark went from abandoning the journey to writing one of the Gospels. In
2 Timothy, we even see Paul ask for Mark, writing that he was "very useful
for me in ministry" (2 Tim. 4:11). Mark's life was forever changed because
he was given a second chance.

Do you want to be judged by your past mistakes? Why or why not?

When we mess up, where do we go from there? How can we get back into the game?

DISPLAY

Sometimes, it's the hard changes we go through that provide the most clarity. Mark messed up. There are times in all of our lives when we mess up or miss the mark. When this happens, we can feel defeated and not want to show our face again. But Mark chose to put his past mistakes behind him and follow Jesus again. Because of Barnabas's willingness to give him a second chance and his ability to accept a second chance, his life was changed for the better. He led a fruitful life of ministry.

You will be on both sides of this at some point in life. You will need a second chance and be the recipient of uncommon grace, and you will need to show someone else grace. Is there someone in your life now who needs a second chance? Do you need to ask someone for a second chance? Take a moment and pray about these two things right now.

Lord, I pray that I can show uncommon grace to those in my life who may need a second chance. You have shown me so much grace so that I can show it to others. I also pray that when I mess up, I will have the courage to get back up and continue with the mission You have called me to. Bring people into my life who will show me grace and encouragement when I mess up.

Change of Plans

READ ACTS 16:6-10.

*After he had seen the vision, we immediately made
efforts to set out for Macedonia, concluding that God
had called us to preach the gospel to them.*
— Acts 16:10

DISCOVER

Have you ever been on a road trip when your GPS navigated you to an alternate route? I remember on one trip home from the beach, we were confused about why the GPS was taking us off the interstate and onto a small country road. We were on the back roads for at least an hour. It turns out there was a huge accident on the interstate—cars were backed up and we wouldn't have been able to get through. Thank goodness we didn't stay on the interstate!

Paul, Silas, and Timothy had a similar experience when they were trying to head to Asia to spread the gospel. Not just once but twice, God stopped them in their tracks as they attempted to go into Asia. What they couldn't see at the time was that it just wasn't the right timing for them to be in Asia. Or perhaps they weren't who God wanted to use in that moment.

They could have easily become frustrated and decided to keep trying. After all, what they wanted to do was great: they wanted to tell others how to experience Jesus like they had. What could be a better reason for doing something? But they followed the Holy Spirit's leading and changed their plans, and God eventually led them to Europe. This was the place where God wanted to use Paul and Silas all along, even if they didn't understand that at the moment.

When was a time you had different plans than God did? Write about that experience. If you can, look back and notice what God did during that time instead.

Why is it hard to let go of control in our lives? How can we learn to trust God even when we disagree with His plans?

DISPLAY

Sometimes we feel like we are hitting roadblock after roadblock, and it can be hard to understand what God is doing. There will be times in your life when you think you're making a good and right decision, but God says no. Maybe it's a decision about your future college or career. Maybe it's about dating a certain person or working at a Christian camp. No matter what situation you find yourself in, you can trust God's heart, even when you cannot see His hand. It is often in the change of direction that God can receive the most glory in our lives.

God, I am thankful that You know the plans You have for me. As I navigate life, help me to follow Your lead, even when You ask me to change directions. You are God and I am not. Help me to remember to trust You above what I think is best.

WHEN CHANGE IS HARD

WHAT DO YOU DO WHEN YOUR WORLD SEEMS TO FALL APART? WHEN YOU FAIL THE CLASS, YOUR PARENTS GET DIVORCED, CANCER TAKES A LOVED ONE, OR YOUR FRIEND HURTS YOU, IT CAN SEEM HOPELESS. IT'S HARD TO BELIEVE, BUT GOD CAN STILL WORK THROUGH EVEN THE DIFFICULT SEASONS OF LIFE.

He Changes Everything

READ EPHESIANS 4:17-32.

Therefore, I say this and testify in the Lord: You should no longer walk as the Gentiles do, in the futility of their thoughts.
— Ephesians 4:17

DISCOVER

Some things in life look completely different once they've gone through a change. For example, a caterpillar turns into a butterfly, and the green leaves of summer turn to orange and red in the fall. Even ladybugs only turn into the red and black polka-dotted insects we recognize after they have experienced a huge change in their life—young ladybugs look completely different!

Once we have an encounter with Jesus, He begins changing us to be like Him. This takes work and effort, but if you truly seek Him, God allows you to be slowly transformed into someone much different than who you were before you entered into a relationship with Jesus. We call this process *sanctification.*

Part of the change that happens in sanctification is we put our old selves to death—we abandon the things that go against what God would have for us. This can be difficult. The sins or behaviors that we have held onto for so long are not going to automatically disappear when we begin a relationship with Jesus. We must work at it. We must give it to God. We must ask Him to help us change.

It's not easy, but it's worth it. Let me repeat that: it is worth it. The hard changes that you need to make to grow closer to Jesus and reflect His heart are more than worth the struggle. With the help of the Holy Spirit, you can let go of the sins that weigh you down.

Take a minute to pray about what things God needs to help you change in your life. Is there a secret sin that you have not let go of? Is there an attitude you have against someone in your life that you need to give to God? Pray that God will bring those things to your mind right now. Write your prayer below.

Who can help you in your journey? Think of a parent, leader, or friend who can come alongside you as you begin to make the necessary changes in your life, and consider reaching out to him or her today. Write this person's name below and how he or she can help you.

DISPLAY

Our old selves want us to stay the same; however, God calls us to change. As God leads you to start some changes in your life, there are a few disciplines that will help you live for Jesus.

It starts with a committed time in the Word and with prayer. I would recommend using your Bible, a journal, and your favorite pens and highlighters to get into God's Word daily. The practice will transform you like nothing else can (see Heb. 4:12).

Another important practice is accountability. This could look like making sure the friends in your inner circle are people who will encourage you in your faith. It could also look like having someone whose faith is more mature than yours who will encourage and support you in your walk with Jesus.

Come up with a plan for daily Bible reading and prayer, reach out to the people God brings to your mind to help you in the journey, and watch the change He begins in your life.

Lord, thank You for saving me. Thank You for inviting me into Your story. As I grow in You, help me to put to death the things in my life that pull me away from You. In their place, let me put on the things that You love. I pray that You will give me the strength and wisdom to make changes in my life. Thank You that I do not have to do this alone.

All In

READ LUKE 1:26-38.

"See, I am the Lord's servant," said Mary. "May it happen to me as you have said." Then the angel left her.
— Luke 1:38

DISCOVER

I have been blessed to have two children, and they both have been the most welcome changes in my life. There is nothing that will alter your life like a baby who wakes up all night and needs her diaper changed. Even though my husband and I planned to have kids, it was still a bit of a shock when the reality came.

Mary was a teenager, and she wasn't planning on having kids quite yet. She was engaged to Joseph, but they weren't yet married. When God told her she was going to be pregnant, her world suddenly changed. This pregnancy could have cost her more than discomfort and humiliation. In her culture, she could have been given the death penalty for what was thought to be adultery. Mary could have tried to beg God to choose someone else. After all, this pregnancy would mean she would constantly face the judgmental eyes of everyone around her. Her relationship with Joseph would be different. However, saying no to God would mean a rejection of what He was asking her to do.

As difficult and dangerous as this change in her life would be, her response was perfect. She said, "See, I am the Lord's servant. May it happen to me as you have said" (Luke 1:38). She didn't tell the angel "You must have the wrong girl." She didn't try to pawn the responsibility off on someone else. She humbly told the angel that she was all in. If it was what God wanted, it was what she wanted too, even if that meant her life didn't look like she thought it would.

Write about a time when you felt God telling you to do something. Did you follow through? Why or why not?

Spend some time praying about the things in life that God wants you to do. These can be as simple as sharing Jesus with a friend or as big as devoting your life to full-time ministry. Write out those things here.

DISPLAY

God asks us to do hard things. God may call you to overseas missions or He may ask you to sit with the lonely student at lunch. He may ask you to give your life to full-time ministry or He may ask you to share the love of Jesus with the people on your sports team. But chances are, we won't have an angel come tell us exactly what God's mission is for our life. Most of the time, it looks like taking small steps of obedience. The consistent small steps of obedience over time end up helping us run the race that God has set before us.

We need to follow the example of Mary and put our yes on the table. We can do hard things. When God asks us to do something, He will help us through it. What is God asking you to say yes to today?

God, You are so good. Thank You for providing ways for us to join in on what You are doing in the world. Help me to make daily small steps of obedience so that when You ask me to do something big, I will gladly and humbly put my yes on the table. Help me to be sensitive to Your leading as I walk with You.

Day by Day

READ 2 CORINTHIANS 4:7-18.

Therefore we do not give up. Even though our outer person is being destroyed, our inner person is being renewed day by day.
— 2 Corinthians 4:16

DISCOVER

In a world full of change and uncertainty, there are a few certain things. One of those things is that there will be affliction in our lives. From stubbing our toes to sunburn to more serious afflictions like cancer or persecution, we will face troubles in this life.

Paul was no stranger to struggle. In his life, he saw beatings, shipwrecks, hunger, thirst, sleeplessness, and many other hardships (see 2 Cor. 11: 23-28). At times he didn't just ride the struggle bus—he drove it!

Paul had so much going against him that he could have easily given up or fallen into despair. Yet, he knew that the temporary challenges he faced didn't compare to the glory that awaited him in eternity. Since he understood what challenges felt like and knew the closeness of the Lord through them, Paul could guide others in how to be renewed day by day. He knew that the worst things that could happen to us on earth can't compare to the goodness that awaits us in heaven.

On top of this, God does some incredible work in our lives through our pain. I can't explain exactly how it works, but God does something beautiful to our hearts—our "inner person," as Paul called it—when we are facing struggles. We learn a closeness with Him that doesn't come in any other way.

How have you seen God through your past struggles?

How can you fix your eyes on Jesus even during the trials you find yourself in?

DISPLAY

Chances are, you have felt like Paul at some point. The struggles seem to pile up, and you don't know where to go or what to do. Recently, I went through one of the hardest times of my life. I had been diagnosed with cancer, and as part of my cancer treatment, I had to go through chemotherapy. The chemo caused my hair to fall out. It also made me tired and sick. Then I had to go through several surgeries on the path to healing. But something amazing happened. While externally, I was in pain and my body seemed to be wasting away, I was being renewed spiritually. I am a much stronger person because of my health journey. The lessons I learned about God and His faithfulness could only have been learned through such pain.

Pain and struggle aren't fun, but God renews us during that time. He reveals things about Himself beautifully and powerfully.

The next time you find yourself in a trial, just remember two things: first, God can teach you through the pain, and second, these struggles won't even matter once you see Jesus face to face.

God, what a gift You are. Thank You for the trials I will face. I pray that You will do what only You can do through the struggles I face. Teach me the lessons You have for me and help me to remember that life with You is always better.

I love You!

Through the Fire

READ JAMES 1:2-18.

Consider it a great joy, my brothers and sisters, whenever you experience various trials, because you know that the testing of your faith produces endurance. And let endurance have its full effect, so that you may be mature and complete, lacking nothing.
— James 1:2-4

DISCOVER

The Bible challenges us to consider it joy when we find ourselves in a challenging season. This doesn't mean we have to enjoy it. It just means that when we see things through God's perspective, we can find joy even when we go through hard things that test our faith.

It's sort of like eating vegetables. Some people love them, while for others they're a challenge. We all know that eating veggies is good for us, but sometimes our parents have to force us to eat them. However, unlike eating vegetables, God doesn't let us face hardships just because they're good for us. He allows us to go through seasons of challenge because it makes us mature and complete in Him.

There is just something unexplainable that God does in our spiritual life when we go through the hard things. It is in the tough times that we are forced to rely on His strength and wisdom. The testing of our faith produces endurance in our lives.

Think of it like this: the gold in the beautiful jewelry we see in stores goes through an intense refining period before it ever goes behind the display case. This refining period consists of fire, heat, melting, and pouring. If the gold didn't go through that process, it wouldn't be as beautiful and valuable to us. The same kind of process happens in our life. We can rejoice in the trials because we know that God can use them to mold us into the people He has called us to be.

What trials are you facing right now? How can you rejoice despite or even because of these trials?

Look back at the trials you have already faced. How are you stronger and wiser because of them?

DISPLAY

Sometimes, when we face trials, we don't know which direction to go. Thankfully, we have a promise in Scripture that can help us as we pray. James 1:5 tells us that if we lack wisdom, we can ask God and He will give it to us. If you do not know which college to go to—ask God for wisdom. If you don't know how to handle friendship drama—ask God for wisdom. At the same time, don't be discouraged if you ask Him once and all your questions aren't answered. Jesus also tells us to keep on asking God for what we need (see Luke 11:5-13). He has given us a promise that we can claim even in our trials.

Father, thank You for loving me, even when my faith is tested. Thank You for walking with me through the hard things in life. It is because of the hard things in life that I can grow and mature into the person You want me to be.

Bring it to the Light

READ 1 JOHN 1:5-10.

If we confess our sins, he is faithful and righteous to forgive
us our sins and to cleanse us from all unrighteousness.
— 1 John 1:9

DISCOVER

Here is the truth: we all sin. There is no way to get around that. We are flawed and human, and we make mistakes. Sometimes those mistakes become habits that are hard to break. Jesus wants better for you. He wants you to live a victorious life. However, the destructive habits in our lives can be difficult to break.

You may be good at hiding your sin, but even if your parents, friends, and teachers have no idea what you're doing, God does. He still chooses to love you despite your sin, but His desire is for you to break free from the sins that bring you down. Chances are, that secret sin causes you anxiety, affects your relationships, and hinders your most important relationship—the one you have with Jesus.

The secret sins we hold on to lose their power when we bring them into the light. When we confess our sins and shortcomings to God, we can be restored in our relationship with Him and not hindered by the weight of shame and guilt we carry around.

Be honest with yourself: What sins do you find yourself fighting regularly? How are they affecting your relationships?

Who can come alongside you to keep you accountable? Write the names of one or two people below.

DISPLAY

You can confess your sin today. First, spend some time in honest prayer today asking God to make the changes in your life to put you in right standing with Him. Next, tell someone you trust. This might be a parent, mentor, church leader, or friend. Whomever you choose to help you in the journey, make sure it is someone who loves Jesus and wants to see you grow in your relationship with Him.

Lord, thank You for loving me despite my sin. I come before You today open to making the changes that I need to make to live fully for You. Please bring the sin in my life to the forefront of my mind so that I can confess it, ask for forgiveness, and turn to follow You.

The Power of Story

READ GENESIS 37.

Judah said to his brothers, ". . . Come on, let's sell him to the Ishmaelites and not lay a hand on him, for he is our brother, our own flesh," and his brothers agreed.
— Genesis 37:26-27

DISCOVER

There is power in a story. A good (and true) story has the power to change our perspective and help us see things in a different light. The story of Joseph is one of those stories. He was put in a lot of difficult situations, one after another—so many that we might have a hard time imagining so many horrible things happening to a single person. However, God was good through it all, and He had a wonderful plan for Joseph and his family. Joseph's story shows us how, despite the temporary trials we may face, we can trust that God has a purpose and plan.

Joseph was the favorite kid. His dad loved him more than his other sons and showed Joseph much favoritism, such as making him a special robe. His brothers were fully aware that Joseph was the favorite, and they hated him because of it.

One day, Joseph had a dream where his brothers and father were all bowing down to him. He could have kept that dream to himself, but he decided to share the dream with his family. It probably wasn't the best move to rub that dream in their faces—it made the sibling rivalry take a dark turn, and the brothers decided to kill Joseph! At the last minute, however, they decided that they would instead sell him to some traders who were passing through. What a reversal—one day he dreams of his brothers bowing down to him, and the next day he is being sold into slavery by these same brothers.

What abrupt changes have you seen in your own life? How did you deal with them?

How can you keep your eyes on Jesus when people in your life fail you or treat you poorly?

DISPLAY

I am sure the rejection Joseph faced from the people closest to him caused incredible pain. Throughout our lives, we are either going into a storm, in the middle of a storm, or coming out of a storm. Life will always have storms that come along. However, from the story of Joseph (which we will look at over the next few days), we learn that no matter what we go through, God is still with us. We can trust that no matter what changes come our way, God has a plan. Joseph did not know how things would turn out in his life, but He could trust God along the way.

In the space below or on a separate piece of paper, draw a timeline of your life. Mark the important dates and things that happened along the way. Reflect on how God brought you through those things and how He is with you still today.

Father, You have a plan for my life that is better than anything I could dream of. When things happen that go against what I think my plan should be, remind me to trust You. When people or things fail me, I may want to retaliate. Help me to see You during the struggle and trust that You have a plan.

MEMORY VERSES

CONSIDER IT A GREAT JOY,
MY BROTHERS AND SISTERS,
WHENEVER YOU EXPERIENCE
VARIOUS TRIALS, BECAUSE
YOU KNOW THAT THE TESTING
OF YOUR FAITH PRODUCES
ENDURANCE. AND LET
ENDURANCE HAVE ITS FULL
EFFECT, SO THAT YOU MAY BE
MATURE AND COMPLETE,
LACKING NOTHING.

— JAMES 1:2-4

You're Kidding Me!

READ GENESIS 39.

"No one in this house is greater than I am. He has withheld nothing from me except you, because you are his wife. So how could I do this immense evil, and how could I sin against God?"
— *Genesis 39:9*

DISCOVER

After being sold into slavery, Joseph ended up in Egypt working in the home of a man named Potiphar. The Lord was with Joseph and blessed him, even though his circumstances were less than ideal. Eventually, Joseph became the overseer of Potiphar's house.

Joseph's master also had a wife. We do not know her name, but we do know that she took notice of Joseph. Day after day, she made sexual advances toward him, and Joseph consistently refused out of respect for God and Potiphar. One day, when she felt the timing was right, she tried again. Being full of integrity, Joseph refused and ran away. However, she grabbed his garment—probably a robe of some kind—and as he escaped, it tore off in her hands. Potiphar's wife used Joseph's clothing to twist reality. She claimed that Joseph had tried to take advantage of her and that her screaming made him run away without his clothes. As a result, Joseph was thrown in prison.

Joseph did the right thing, but he still ended up in jail. He went from a position of authority in his master's house to wrongly accused of an crime he didn't commit. Doing the right thing doesn't always mean that things will go well.

However, not even prison could separate Joseph from the love and care of God, and he soon found favor with the prison guard. Eventually, he was put in the position of overseeing all the prisoners. The prison guard trusted Joseph so much that he didn't even pay attention to anything Joseph did.

In your opinion, what made Joseph able to turn down Potiphar's wife?

How can you make God-honoring decisions in your life?

When have you made the right decision but had a difficult result still come of it?

DISPLAY

Our integrity is measured by what we do when no one is looking. When you're taking a test you didn't study for and you can see the smartest kid's answers, what do you do? When your parents have set certain family rules, but they aren't around to know whether you are following the rules or not, what do you do?

Making the decision that honors God isn't always easy, but it's always best. It may mean failing your test or missing out on what your friends are doing. But just like the Lord was with Joseph, He is with you, too. You don't have to make these decisions alone. God can give you the strength to make the right choices, no matter what the outcome may be. The closer we are to God, the easier it will be to make a decision that honors Him.

Decide now that you want to be the same person when no one is looking as you are when all eyes are on you. God will bless this decision as He shapes your character and gives you strength.

Lord, thank You for being with me during both my highs and my lows. I pray that I will be so close to You that You will give me the strength to make decisions that glorify You, despite what the outcome may be. I desire to honor You and give You glory in everything that I do.

In the Waiting

READ GENESIS 40.

"But when all goes well for you, remember that I was with you. Please show kindness to me by mentioning me to Pharaoh, and get me out of this prison."
— Genesis 40:14

DISCOVER

Joseph was in prison for a crime he didn't commit when one day, two new prisoners arrived—the king's cupbearer and baker—and both of them had some crazy dreams that they couldn't interpret the meaning of. When Joseph found out, he interpreted their dreams for them. His one request was that they would remember him. He wanted a way out of prison and into a more normal life.

Three days later, the cupbearer was restored to his former position. But despite Joseph's request, the cupbearer forgot him. He didn't tell anyone about Joseph and his ability to interpret dreams.

Although there was good coming Joseph's way, he may not have seen that in the moment. If I were Joseph, I would probably have felt discouraged. He had spent his life making the right decisions only to be stuck in jail. He finally thought his circumstances were going to change, but they didn't.

Once again, Joseph's life shows us that there is value in waiting. Make no mistake about it—waiting for your circumstances to change is difficult. However, we know the One who holds the future in His hands. This means that even when things aren't going our way, we can rest in the confidence that God is still in control. Nothing in our lives or anywhere else happens outside of His knowledge or allowance.

Read Romans 8:28. How does this verse encourage you to stay faithful even when things aren't going the way you thought they should?

What are steps you can take to switch your mindset when you find yourself feeling discouraged or defeated?

DISPLAY

We may find ourselves in a place where we feel defeated. We desperately want our circumstances to change, but they don't. We make all the right decisions, and yet we don't experience what we are hoping for and we feel stuck in our circumstances. It's in those moments that we need to trust that God is in control of all the changes in our lives. He loves us more than you could ever imagine.

Read Romans 8:28, Ephesians 1:11, and John 10:29. Memorize one (or all) of these verses to call back to memory when you need a reminder of God's love and His control over all circumstances.

Lord, thank You for loving me amid the circumstances I find myself in. I can trust that You have a plan and a purpose for me, even when I feel stuck. Help me to trust You, even when I feel defeated.

DAY 19

Finally!

READ GENESIS 41.

*So Pharaoh said to Joseph, "Since God has made all this
known to you, there is no one as discerning and wise as you are.
You will be over my house, and all my people will obey
your commands. Only I, as king, will be greater than you."*
— Genesis 41:39-40

DISCOVER

Two years after Joseph correctly interpreted the cupbearer's dreams, he was still in prison. Two years of trusting God for something better. Then, one day, Pharaoh had a dream that woke him up. He couldn't interpret what this dream full of cows could mean, and he needed to find out. He started asking around. No one could tell him what this dream meant.

Then, the cupbearer remembered Joseph. He remembered how Joseph had interpreted not only his dreams but also the dreams of the baker. Immediately, Pharaoh called for Joseph. As Joseph stood before Pharaoh, instead of taking the credit himself, he gave credit to God.

The dream was a warning from God that there would be seven years of wonderful harvest, followed by seven years of famine. Pharaoh needed to prepare for the famine so there would be food for the people once it happened.

Because of what Pharaoh saw in Joseph, he appointed Joseph to be over his house and in charge of all of his people. Joseph went from wasting away in prison to becoming the second in command over all of Egypt. He spent the next seven years working hard so that when the famine came, they still had food. God's plan for Joseph continued to unfold, and as we'll see tomorrow, it did so in ways Joseph could have never imagined.

Have you ever experienced an obvious blessing from God after a hard season of disappointment? Explain.

When you use a gift that God has given you, what steps can you take to make sure that God gets the credit and glory rather than building up yourself and your own ego?

DISPLAY

God's plan finally began to reveal itself, but it was only after years of Joseph trusting and waiting. Sometimes, it's hard to see what God has planned for us when we're in the middle of the valley. Psalm 23:4 tells us that God is with us even when we walk through the darkest valleys. It is important to notice here that we will still need to walk through the valleys—God won't always make the difficulties go away. Joseph is a prime example of that. He spent time walking through dark days, but God was with him every step of the way. The mountaintops are much sweeter when we have trusted God all along the way.

Lord, thank You for never leaving my side. Even when I can't see You moving in my life, I can trust that You are. Help me praise You in the waiting and praise You when I see You moving. I could never do anything to earn Your love, but I am so thankful for it.

Reunited

READ GENESIS 45.

"God sent me ahead of you to establish you as a remnant within the land and to keep you alive by a great deliverance."
— Genesis 45:7

DISCOVER

Eventually, just like Pharaoh's dream had predicted, famine struck the land. But thanks to Joseph, Egypt was prepared. As food became scarce throughout the nearby regions, word spread that there was food in Egypt. So, Jacob sent his sons there to buy grain so they wouldn't starve.

All of Joseph's brothers—other than his youngest brother, Benjamin—went to Egypt to buy grain. Since Joseph was in charge of all the food distribution, his brothers came before him to ask for food. Joseph immediately recognized them, but they didn't realize they were speaking to their brother. This is how another of Joseph's dreams came true—the one he had as a boy. The one that caused his brothers to sell him into slavery.

After some time, Joseph finally revealed himself to his brothers—and then he had a decision to make. He could have easily turned away from his brothers after how they treated him. Instead, he chose to forgive them. In fact, he not only forgave them but he offered Egypt's best to their family. Joseph had the wisdom to see that all the hard changes that he had gone through brought him to the position he was in. It was God's provision for his family all along.

Why do you think it's so difficult to forgive others? What do you see as the benefits of forgiveness?

'

When we forgive, it changes our hearts. Why do you think that is?

DISPLAY

After everything that Joseph went through, he chose to forgive. In our world where cancel culture is a norm, offering grace and forgiveness is the exception rather than the rule. However, when we choose to forgive those who have hurt us, it changes our hearts.

Jesus gave us the ultimate example of this forgiveness. After leading a perfect life, He willingly died on the cross to offer us forgiveness and a chance to be reconciled to God. This example helps us to see that we can offer forgiveness to those who have hurt us.

Is there someone in your life who you need to forgive? Unfortunately, because of sin, we will all experience times of hurt. But when we choose to forgive instead of carrying a grudge, we are more like Jesus. Take some time to think about those that have wronged you. If you have never forgiven them, I pray that you will make that decision. There is freedom in forgiveness.

Lord, thank You that You chose to forgive me, a sinner. I know there will be times in life when I will be in a position to choose forgiveness. I pray that You would help me to forgive others, as You have forgiven me. Help me lead by Your example.

SOME THINGS NEVER CHANGE

AS MUCH CHANGE AS WE WILL INEVITABLY FACE IN LIFE, WE CAN REST ASSURED THAT GOD WILL NEVER CHANGE. AS WE NAVIGATE THE VARIOUS SEASONS OF CHANGE IN OUR LIVES, WE CAN BE CERTAIN THAT GOD AND HIS LOVE WILL NEVER CHANGE. HE'S THE CONSTANT IN OUR EVER-CHANGING LIVES.

Yesterday, Today, and Forever

READ HEBREWS 13:7-19.

Jesus Christ is the same yesterday, today, and forever.
— Hebrews 13:8

DISCOVER

Do you remember when everyone was doing the floss? (The dance, not the kind you use to clean your teeth!) Thank goodness that trend changed. When I was a teenager, the trend was to curl your bangs and make them as big as possible. I could show you some embarrassing pictures! Thankfully, that trend has also changed.

In Hebrews 13, we see a very important truth. Jesus is the same yesterday, today, and forever. In a world that is constantly changing, we can cling to the truth that Jesus doesn't change. Let that sink in. Jesus is the same yesterday, today, and tomorrow.

Why is this truth important?

1. It helps you to recognize false teaching. Thanks to the internet, we are constantly being told how to live. New trends and fads are shoved into our faces daily. We can use Jesus's unchanging nature to help us recognize whether or not something is of God.

2. You can trust Jesus and know Him. The promises that Jesus made don't change. We know that if Jesus said it, we can believe it. There will never be anything that happens to make Jesus's promises change. The gospel doesn't change, even when it seems like everything else does.

3. It provides stability in our lives. Although all our other relationships have the ability to let us down, we know that our relationship with Jesus never will. Knowing this truth can ground us. Everything else can tip and turn, but we can stand firm on the unchanging nature of Jesus.

How does the truth that Jesus never changes encourage you as a believer?

How does your life reflect the truth of Jesus's unchanging nature?

DISPLAY

How we live our lives can change because Jesus does not. Where the people in the time of Hebrews were questioning whether food regulations and rituals save a person or not, we see that Jesus is the only one who saves. That never changes.

Line up the things you see on social media with Scripture. If something goes against what the Bible says, you know that it's not worth your time. If you don't know what the Bible says, look it up or ask a trusted spiritual mentor. There will be many ideas that appear to be true but are slightly twisted versions of the truth. Since the Bible never changes, we can use it to discern whether or not something is true or right.

Lord, in a world that is constantly changing, You never do. Thank You for consistently loving me. As I hear about the latest trends or new things the world says are true, help me to line everything up with Your Word. If You said it, we can believe it.

One Constant

READ ECCLESIASTES 3:1-15.

I know that everything God does will last forever; there is no adding to it or taking from it. God works so that people will be in awe of him.
— Ecclesiastes 3:14

DISCOVER

We work so hard to control all our surroundings so that things will be perfect, but the truth is that we can't even come close to reaching that goal. Our efforts to control and build a perfect life will fall short every time. Our white shoes become dirty. A friendship becomes toxic. That A we had in English plummets with one bad test grade.

Life is full of change. We change clothes every day. We change classes, and sometimes we have to change where we live. Our friendships and passions change. Ironically, change is a constant in life.

Just as the leaves change color, there is a season for everything in life, yet what God does endures the test of time. He doesn't change as our seasons of life do. He is consistent and stable, and He has a firm foundation on which we can rest. He is the same yesterday, today, and forever (see Heb. 13:8).

Because God is the same and doesn't experience change, that means:

His love doesn't change.
His protection doesn't change.
His character don't change.
His power doesn't change.

Even though almost everything in life will experience change, our respect and awe for God must never change. He is the constant in life.

What changes in your life have you noticed in the last year? How did these changes affect you?

How can we know what things need to change and what things do not need to change?

DISPLAY

You are most likely around hundreds of people each day. From school and church to sports and other activities, you encounter people regularly. These people whom you encounter all have different changes that they are experiencing in life. We never really know what the people around us are going through. It can be a challenge to show them the constant love of Jesus in the midst of a changing world. When others see that our faith isn't shaken when change comes, they'll be curious as to why. Then you have the privilege of sharing with them about the constant love of Jesus, the love that never changes. How would you explain the unchanging nature of Jesus to a friend?

Lord, thank You for being constant when everything else changes. I am thankful I can count on You. You are so good. Help me to show the people in my circles the incredible love that You have so freely given to me.

Think About This

READ PHILIPPIANS 4:4-9.

*Don't worry about anything, but in everything, through prayer
and petition with thanksgiving, present your requests to God.
And the peace of God, which surpasses all understanding,
will guard your hearts and minds in Christ Jesus.*
— Philippians 4:6-7

DISCOVER

Sometimes life just isn't what we thought it would be. I know you've been there. I've been there too. We mess up. Sometimes those closest to us mess up. We have all been in a position that feels heavy; sometimes it feels so heavy that it could crush us. Our mind starts spiraling, and before we know it, we've worked ourselves up into a panic. It is so hard to know how to stop the destructive spiral of our thoughts and emotions.

Thankfully, God gives us an uncomplicated way to attack the anxious thoughts that creep into our minds. It's spelled out for us here in Philippians 4:4-9. Paul knew what it was like to struggle. He had spent countless hours in jail. He had been shipwrecked and beaten up. Still, he experienced the peace that we all want—the peace of God. Here is how he said that we can experience it, too:

1. Rejoice no matter the circumstance.
2. Let your gentleness be known to everyone.
3. Pray continuously.
4. Have a heart filled with gratitude.

That is it! Seriously, it's that simple. If you want the peace that can only come from God, this is the recipe. I've been through some dark days, but in the darkness, I found peace that could only come from Jesus. Jesus offers the gift of peace during our trials, and that never changes.

What situations do you need to give to God today?

How does your thought life match the principles listed in Philippians 4:8? If they don't match up, how can you shift your thinking?

DISPLAY

It's easy to focus on what is wrong in life. I have been known to spiral down a path of negativity, and I know I'm not the only one. But God tells us in His Word that there is a better way. We need to focus on the good, because the things we set our minds on will transform our thoughts and our actions. Philippians 4:8 gives us a list of attributes that will transform a mindset of negativity into one that is God-honoring and hopeful.

Spend some time meditating and praying over the issues you're struggling with. Then, using the list of attributes in Philippians 4:8 (see below), find something from each attribute to praise God for.

God is...

True
Honorable
Just
Pure
Lovely
Commendable
Excellent
Worthy of praise

God doesn't want you to live a life of anxiety and stress—He wants to give you peace. We do our part when we focus our minds and hearts on the right things.

Lord, thank You for giving us a blueprint for peace. Help me to rejoice in all circumstances and to find peace that only You can give. You are so good to me. I pray that I can keep my mind on things of You and not on the things of the world.

Hope Fulfilled

READ MALACHI 3:1-6.

"Because I, the Lord, have not changed, you
descendants of Jacob have not been destroyed."
— Malachi 3:6

DISCOVER

Each book of the Old Testament points beautifully to a Messiah, whom we know today as Jesus. The Israelites had been hoping for and awaiting the arrival of the Messiah for centuries. During those years, God sent prophets to declare messages to His people about the Messiah and how to live in preparation for His arrival. Malachi was one of these prophets, and he lived around four hundred years before Jesus was born.

In Malachi 3, we see a prophecy of two messengers: one who will go before the Messiah to announce His coming and one who is the Messiah Himself. The first messenger was John the Baptist, and the second was Jesus. Malachi foretold that the coming Messiah would be like both a refiner's fire and a launderer's soap. Basically, he was saying that once Jesus arrived, He would make us new. It wouldn't necessarily be a pleasant experience, and it would probably even cause some pain. But the end result would be that He would make us clean and pure.

Thankfully, we live on the other side of that prophecy. Unlike Malachi and the people he was prophesying to, we know Jesus. But the promise of the prophecy still applies to us who live on the other side of the resurrection. Until the day that Jesus returns, we can endure, because He does not change. He is the same yesterday, today, and forever. We no longer live in anticipation of a savior; our hope has arrived, and we can known our Savior personally.

How can the prophecies of the Old Testament that have already been fulfilled bring you comfort?

In what ways does the unchanging nature of God allow you to trust Him more?

DISPLAY

We live in a day when we don't have to wonder who the Messiah is: we can know for sure that Jesus is the One whom the prophecies were about. This should bring us hope and peace. His birth drastically changed everything, and that means it should change everything in our lives, too. If you are struggling in some way today, find a note card or piece of paper and write the word "hope" on one side. On the other side, write a verse or two of Old Testament Scripture that points toward the coming Messiah and has been fulfilled in Jesus. A great place to start would be Isaiah 53:5. However, there are literally dozens of great options to choose from. Keep this card or paper nearby today and glance at it when you need a reminder that God keeps His promises and that our hope has been fulfilled in Jesus.

Lord, I'm so thankful for the fulfilled prophecies of Jesus's birth. Thank You for coming to this earth to live as a man. You didn't have to do that, and I'm forever grateful that You did. Because of what You did on the cross, I can have eternal life with You. Do in my heart what only You can do.

Origin Story

READ GENESIS 1:26-31.

So God created man in his own image; he created him
in the image of God; he created them male and female.
— Genesis 1:27

DISCOVER

I love a good origin story, and nothing beats the story of the creation of the world. First, God created everything from nothing. Then He brought the world to life and made everything that exists. The very last things He made were man and woman, then He called His creation "very good."

Today, we often feel like we can control or change every area of our lives, from our style to our relationships. Some people even feel they can change their gender. Yes, there are some things in life we can and should change, but our gender is not one of them. We see in Scripture that God designed us in His image as either male or female. And as He said in the beginning, this is very good.

Whether they realize it or not, when people decide to experiment with switching genders, they are saying that they know better than God. They are saying that the way God made them isn't right, so they are going to take matters into their own hands and fix it. The truth is, each of us were created as we are with purpose and intention. God didn't make any mistakes when He created us.

God's Word is clear, and standing on God's truth can make us very unpopular. However, we should never insult, judge, or make fun of someone who is struggling with his or her identity. Our response should always be to come alongside that person and lovingly point him or her to Jesus's love and His Word. When we live by God's design, there is freedom. However, when we go against God's design, it will often lead to increased pain and struggle.

How have you ever been tempted to go against God's plan for your life? When you have, what was the result?

In an ever-changing world, how can you help give hope to those struggling with gender issues?

DISPLAY

Gender identity issues are spiritual issues. Do you trust that God is who He says He is? Do you trust that His Word is true? If you do, you will see that God loves you just the way you are. He desires good for you. He has a plan for your life, and that plan is not for you to stay stuck in sin and shame. Even though He loves you as you are, He has no intention of leaving you that way. He desires to transform you.

Is there an area in your life where you feel stuck? Take some time right now to pray about that. Ask God to help you submit yourself fully to Him and to live for Him.

Lord, thank You for Your Word. Thank You for creating me just the way You did. I know that I am fearfully and wonderfully made and that it was not an accident. I pray that I will be able to offer hope to a confused world as I love my friends and family. In a world that is desperate for answers and solutions, I know that the answer is You.

Remarkably, Wondrously

READ PSALM 139:13-16.

I will praise you because I have been remarkably and wondrously made.
Your works are wondrous, and I know this very well.
— Psalm 139:14

DISCOVER

Have you ever hated a certain body part or personality trait that you have? I sure have. We can get so down on ourselves because we don't measure up to what we think we should look like or how we think we need to act. It's easy to fall into the comparison trap and feel like we don't measure up.

The truth is that you were made with purpose and intention. You are fearfully and wonderfully made by the Creator of the universe. The same God who made the platypus, the angler fish, and the emperor penguin made you. He made your personality, no matter how big it is. He made your quirks, gifts, and talents, no matter how obscure they are. And although He cares about the emperor penguin, His care for you goes so much deeper (see Matt. 10:31).

There are times in life when things happen that make us wonder how God could possibly love us. Sometimes our sin is so great that we doubt that God would have enough love to forgive us. The good news is that nothing, not one thing, could change the love, care, and value that God has for you. Nothing can separate us from God's love (see Rom. 8:38-39).

Romans 5:8 says that "God proves his own love for us in that while we were still sinners, Christ died for us." Not only are you remarkable and wondrously made, but Jesus loves you so much that despite your sin, He died for you.

Look up the following verses. Write down how God sees you.

- **1 Peter 2:9**

- **2 Corinthians 5:17**

- **Romans 8:16-17**

How does knowing these truths about how God sees you change your view of yourself?

DISPLAY

You are remarkably and wondrously made, and so is everyone else. What this tells me is that the way we treat people matters. As humans, we were made in the image of God. This is huge. We all have a purpose here on earth. That kid that always sits by himself at lunch and pokes holes in the cafeteria apple . . . he's fearfully and wonderfully made. The kid who doesn't always understand social cues and stands so close to you that you smell her breath . . . you guessed it, she's fearfully and wonderfully made.

What would happen if we treated all people the way God sees them? How would our schools, teams, churches, and families change if we showed people that we see them as valuable and loved? The bottom line is that you are made with purpose and intention, and so are the people around you. Nothing can change that.

It's humbling to think that before I was even born, You knew me, loved me, and chose to create me. I'm honored that You saw fit to make me the way You did. Help me to know my worth in You and then share that hope and love with the world.

I WILL PRAISE YOU BECAUSE
I HAVE BEEN REMARKABLY
AND WONDROUSLY MADE.
YOUR WORKS ARE WONDROUS,
AND I KNOW THIS VERY WELL.

— Psalm 139:14

MEMORY
VERSE

Every Knee Will Bow

READ PHILIPPIANS 2:1-11.

For this reason God highly exalted him and gave him the name that is above every name, so that at the name of Jesus every knee will bow — in heaven and on earth and under the earth — and every tongue will confess that Jesus Christ is Lord, to the glory of God the Father.
— Philippians 2:9-11

DISCOVER

There are several inevitabilities in life, such as pop quizzes, a broken ice cream machine at that particular fast food place, and a long grocery store line on the day you are in a hurry. These are just little speed bumps in life. However, there is a very real guarantee that we need to pay attention to.

God has highly exalted Jesus and given Him the name above every name because He did what we could never do: He took His position as God and humbled Himself, took on human form, lived a perfect life, and in obedience, died on the cross for our sins. Because of this, God has exalted Him above all.

Because of this, the Bible says that at the right time, every knee will bow, and every tongue will confess that Jesus is Lord. This includes not only the people who know and love Jesus but also the people who do not believe, have not heard of, or even hate Jesus. There will be a day when every person will claim Jesus as Lord, either in joyful celebration or with regret and despair. This is a guarantee that cannot be changed.

This is a challenge for us to examine our hearts. It also gives us a mission and purpose for how we spend the time we have in life. The promise of verses 9-11 should propel us to live out verses 1-5 and make heaven crowded.

Is your life pointing others to Jesus or away from Jesus? How so?

How does the guarantee that every single person will eventually call Jesus Lord affect the way you live today?

Living like Jesus has always been countercultural. Verse 2 tells us that as believers, we need to be unified by having the same mind and the same love. When we are at odds with others, it puts stumbling blocks on the path to loving and serving Jesus. How do we go about being unified? Verse 3 shows us how. When we live our lives putting others first and looking to the needs of others before our own, it leads to unification. When we are unified, we can joyfully reach more people for Jesus. In the divided time we live in, the world needs to see Christians living joyful lives, humble and unified. What is one way you can help create unity in your church today?

Jesus, You are my Savior and Lord. Thank You for saving me and giving me everything that I need for life with You. It is my prayer that I will spend my days humbly living for You. Give me the wisdom and strength to share Your love with the people I interact with each day. Use me to help make heaven crowded.

All Authority

READ MATTHEW 28:18-20.

Jesus came near and said to them, "All authority has been given to me in heaven and on earth."
— Matthew 28:18

DISCOVER

Throughout history, there have been individuals in authority who made some horrible decisions and caused great pain and turmoil for the world, people like Adolf Hitler, Ivan the Terrible, and Emperor Nero, to name a few. You might not have faced authority figures at that level of bad, but we all sometimes grow wary of the people in authority over us. You may have had a bad teacher or principal that makes you not appreciate the authority of others.

In contrast to these men who were hungry for power, think about a leader who is gentle, loving, and kind. One who serves others before Himself. A leader who gives more than He takes. One who values His people and consistently shows forgiveness and compassion. A leader who desires a relationship with us and offers us life. That kind of leader is easy to follow. Following that type of leader is not a burden but a blessing.

In verse 18, we see that all authority has been given to Jesus. Although power can be dangerous in the hands of some, when Jesus is in charge, it's nothing to be afraid of. We can be thankful that He is in charge because we know that He loves and cares for us in a way that we can't even fully comprehend. Thankfully, this authority doesn't change. It's a constant that we can rest in daily.

Why do you think some people have a problem with authority?

How is living under Jesus's authority a gift?

DISPLAY

When the risen Jesus showed Himself to His disciples, most of them worshiped Him, but some doubted He was truly who He said He was. It seemed too good to be true. Could Jesus truly rise from the dead and be face-to-face with them? You can see how maybe it would be hard to believe. Yet, when we encounter Jesus, we are led to worship. Jesus is perfect. He loves and leads us perfectly.

Spend some time today reflecting on the attributes of Jesus. When we see Him for who He is, our lives will be changed. His unchanging nature causes us to change to become more like Him. When we see a clear picture of who Jesus is, it's natural to want to seek and love Him more.

Lord, thank You for being in charge of my life and the lives of others. I am thankful that the truth never changes. Thank You that You are right by my side as I live my life for You. I pray that I will boldly proclaim Your name to a world that desperately needs You. Help me to humbly live out Your plan for me.

Life in Drive

READ MATTHEW 28:18-20.

"Go, therefore, and make disciples of all nations, baptizing them in the name of the Father and of the Son and of the Holy Spirit . . ."
— Matthew 28:19

DISCOVER

As the Gospel of Matthew ends, it also sets us up for a beginning. Because of Jesus and His unchanging authority, we are set in motion and commanded to go into the world to share His message with everyone.

The Great Commission is like our life's ultimate job description. I know I have spent countless hours praying and asking God what He wants me to do in life. Sometimes, I think we can make it more complicated than it needs to be. The "how" and "where" may look different, but when we wonder what God's will is or what He wants us to do in life, this is it. We are to be disciple makers. As we live out the Great Commission, He will open the doors that need to be opened. We don't need to worry about the specifics—we just go.

This is a simple command that requires movement. Sometimes we get paralyzed because we're afraid of making a mistake or are unsure of how to do things right. Think of a parked car. It's extremely difficult to steer a car that's in park. You can push or pull as hard as you want, but it just doesn't go anywhere! To steer the car, you need to put it in drive. At that point, steering a car is simple. You turn the wheel, and the car changes directions—simple as that. In much the same way, we need to put our lives in "drive." When we start sharing with others, God will lead us and direct us to what is next.

How does your life reflect the Great Commission?

What keeps you from going into the world to tell others about Jesus? How can you live a life of boldness for the sake of the gospel?

DISPLAY

As we draw closer to Jesus, He draws closer to us. It's when we are close to Jesus that telling others about Him becomes a natural outpouring of our relationship with Him. After all, we tell people about the things that we're excited about. Whether it's a new coffee shop, video game, or video on the internet, when we find something we love, we want others to know about it. The same thing happens when we fall in love with Jesus. The Great Commission becomes a natural way of living because we can't wait to share how God is teaching and revealing Himself in our lives.

The Great Commission is God's unchanging plan to reach the world. Take the next few minutes and write out what you would say if you were sharing the gospel with someone else.

God, thank You that I get to be a part of Your plan. I pray that my relationship with You would be so tight that telling others about You would be a natural outpouring of my relationship with You. Help me to take the job of being a disciple maker seriously. I want my life to reflect You.

Not Alone

READ MATTHEW 28:18-20.

". . . teaching them to observe everything I have commanded you. And remember, I am with you always, to the end of the age."
— Matthew 28:20

DISCOVER

Have you ever done something that scared you to death? My son is learning to drive this year. The first few times we hit the road, he was terrified. His heart was racing. He was so afraid that he would mess up. The truth, I was a little scared too. My life was in his hands. However, even though he was behind the wheel, I was right beside him the entire time. I was there to redirect him if he was headed in the wrong direction. I was there to help navigate. I was there to encourage him when he messed up (although I'm sure I didn't do this perfectly). I was there to help celebrate when he arrived safely at his destination. He didn't have to learn to drive alone, because I was right there to help him through it.

Jesus calls us to a big task: it can be incredibly scary to attempt to live a life where we put ourselves out there to tell others about Him. The beautiful part is that we don't have to do it alone. He is right there with us. He's there to redirect us, to help us navigate where to go and what to say. He's there to encourage us when we mess up, and He's there to celebrate with us when things go well.

Despite our imperfections, we are still commanded to go. It doesn't matter if we're awkward around people or never know what to say. As we rely on Jesus, He will guide and direct us. We are promised that He is with us—we don't have to go alone. As we go, we go in His unchanging power and authority. As imperfect as we are, He still chooses to use us to spread His name and help create disciples. What a gift we have to serve under the best leader there is!

How does knowing that God is with us encourage you to boldly tell others about Jesus?

Who are some people in your life with whom you need to share the love of Jesus? Write down their names and then write a prayer for them. Ask God for opportunities to share with those people.

DISPLAY

There is never a moment when Jesus isn't with us—this is a comfort that doesn't change. We don't have to be afraid. He is constantly at our side.

Think about that conversation you know you need to have. The one you've been avoiding for months. The one you keep pushing out of your mind. Now, imagine having that conversation with Jesus sitting right beside you. Not only is Jesus with you, but He has given you His power. With Jesus's help, you can do it.

Lord, thank You that I don't have to live life alone. Thank You for always being there with me. No matter what I go through, I can count on the fact that You are with me. I can speak Your name to the people in my life with boldness because You are with me.

Is God Unchanging?

Many of the things that have happened in your lifetime are beyond your control—pieces left over from the world that someone else created and passed down to you, whether you wanted it or not. Because of this, you might experience a steady stream of low-key anxiety and uncertainty. And you might begin to wonder: In a world full of change, does God change?

How would you describe what it means to change?

Change occurs where it is needed. When we change, we grow in either a positive or negative direction. However, our perfect God does not need to grow for the better, nor can His perfection be damaged by mistakes.

God loves us unconditionally, but we see throughout Scripture and His covenants with people that He does sometimes place conditions on His promises. This is important for us to recognize because there are myths that God has changed over time—or at the very least, that He has changed His mind. And there are myths that His Word has changed as well.

Myth 1: God changes as the world changes.

Read Psalm 102:26-27, Malachi 3:6, and James 1:17.

How does Scripture bust myth 1?

God is not the world He created. We can see pieces of His character and love in the good He has given us through His created world and people, but these are only reflections, not perfect representations. God can change the heavens and the earth without changing Himself because He existed before them and exists completely independent of them, even though He is involved in His creation and our lives.

Myth 2: God changes His mind.

Read Job 42:1-2, Psalm 33:11, Proverbs 19:21, Isaiah 46:10, and Ephesians 1:11. Then read the following explanation: "Understanding the distinction between God's unconditional and conditional announcements is the key to answering the question, 'Does God change His mind?' If God issues a decree or makes an oath, then He will not change His mind or deviate from what He has announced. But if He merely announces His intention conditionally (whether explicitly or implicitly), then the response of the recipient may very well move Him to deviate from a stated course of action." [1]

How does Scripture bust myth 2?

God's actions in the world will always align with His nature and His character. We can't understand God's mind, but we do know this: He is omniscient, meaning He knows everything. So, nothing that happens to us or that we decide is news to Him.

Myth 3: God's Word changes as the world changes.

Read Psalm 119:89, Isaiah 40:8, Matthew 24:35, and Hebrews 4:12.

How does Scripture bust myth 3?

The way we apply God's Word to our ever-changing world might be different today than it was in Jesus's day, but God's Word itself doesn't change or become less true over time. God's Word is rooted in Him, and He doesn't change. That God's Word is "living and effective" doesn't mean it changes; rather, the power of God's Word and God's Spirit works in our lives to change us.

When we understand that God doesn't change—and that neither does His will, His mind, or His Word—then we have a strong, steady foundation to stand on in the middle of a chaotic, unpredictable world. We have Him, and that's enough.

1. Robert B. Chisholm, "Does God Change His Mind," Voice (Dallas Theological Seminary), July 7, 2006, https://voice.dts.edu/article/does-god-change-his-mind-robert-b-chisholm-jr/.

How to Handle Change

Knowing that God doesn't change and that He is our anchor can be a steadying truth in a world where we don't always know what to think, believe, feel, or trust. When change comes our way, we can trust who God says He is and that He keeps His promises to work all things for His glory and our ultimate good.

But when we're looking straight into the face of a change—especially a challenging one—we might wonder how to stay grounded in reality when life is so unpredictable, especially when that unpredictability often feels harsh.

Before we look at the practical side of things, let's look at where you are now. Describe how you would feel about each of the following changes. Try to note at least one positive thing and one challenging thing for each one.

Trying Something New
Making a New Friend
Switching Schools or Changing Churches
Moving to a New City, State, or Country

Sometimes, change can be exciting. It can bring a multitude of possibilities and opportunities. Or maybe you've been craving a fresh start. But even good change can unsettle us and pull our hearts and minds away from what matters most.

Here are a few tips to help you stay grounded when life changes:

- Remember, God is for you. Ask Him for help to remain steady, whether the change is hard or exciting.

- Understand that adjusting takes time, and give yourself grace if you struggle.

- Grab a journal and write about how this change makes you feel. If you're more of a verbal processor, read your thoughts aloud or share them with someone you trust.

- Look for the possibilities and opportunities this change brings. How could this actually be a good thing one day, even if it's hard right now?

- If you start to feel stress or pressure weighing you down, take a walk outside. This relaxes your nervous system and helps you think clearer.

- Doing something you love or spending time with someone you care about can improve your mood and even give you a new perspective.

- Don't live in denial or start planning to go back to what you used to do—give the change a fair chance.

- Keep what you can control the same, like your routines. This creates a core of stability that you can return to.

- Consider how you've dealt with change in the past, notice what helped you then, and apply it now.

- Make sure you're taking care of your body by getting rest, eating foods that nourish you, and being physically active.

Above all, embracing change requires us to know and trust God—to trust that He has and will move us where He wants us. By paying attention to what's going on in our heart, mind, and body, we can see where we need to lean into Him, ask others for help, and do something ourselves to not just deal with change but thrive in it.

Engage with God's Word.

lifeway.com/teendevotionals

LOVE AND JUSTICE

CALLED TO THIS

GROWING IN GRATITUDE

GOD WITH US

MADE NEW

LOVE WITH ALL YOUR HEART

RISEN

WISDOM, STATURE, AND FAVOR

BEFORE YOU GO

PRESS PAUSE

CITIZEN OF THE KINGDOM

FINDING YOUR WAY